BARK
up the
RIGHT Tree

Lessons from a
Rescued Dog

Jessie & Ruth Tschudin

ISBN 1-4392-1424-7
Library of Congress Control Number: 2008909353
Printed in US by BookSurge Publishing, Charleston, SC

The Barker

MotoPhoto, Emerson, NJ

Jessie Grace Tschudin

Woof! Woof!

Hi There, Dog Lover!

Woof! *Woof!* I'm so glad you're here. In fact, I'm going into a major tail-spin, and I'm running around like crazy. Such exuberance is typical for me. After all, I'm a dog. A healthy, happy dog named Jessie.

I'm one very lucky pooch! When my original family could no longer keep me, I was adopted by a woman named Ruth and given a wonderful new life. How I wish that every lonesome, heartsick, and abandoned pet could have the same good fortune.

My life story so far is filled with the usual ups and downs, delights and challenges. But in some ways, my story is truly unique. For example, can you believe that it was my name that miraculously saved me? Just stick around, and I'll tell you all about it.

What fun it's been expressing my thoughts and feelings in your language. English is so much more expressive than my everyday *bark-growl-whine* vocabulary. And being able to tap Ruth's brain for all those human insights and juicy details has certainly been enlightening.

But the best part of my journey is that I've learned some valuable lessons along the way. At the end of each chapter, you'll see my paw pointing out these lessons. So take a little time to pause at the "Paws." If you discover some lessons I've overlooked, great! Just write them in and make this book even better.

I'd love to hear from you! You can contact me at my own personal e-mail address: *Jessiesfriends@verizon.net.* I'm always on the lookout for new friends, and I hope you'll be one of them!

Your pal,

Jessie

Table of Contents

Bark up the Right Tree

CHAPTER 1

Will I Ever Stop Hurting?

When things get tough, it's so easy to despair and so hard to imagine ever being well or happy again. I learned this the hard way when I was dropped off at an animal control shelter in Staten Island, New York, by the family I'd lived with my entire life. Someone in my own family, a boy whom I loved and trusted, had emotional problems and started hurting me so much that one of us had to go. Guess who!

It must have been a difficult decision for my loved ones, who had taken such good care of me over the years. They probably thought that bringing me to the shelter was the best thing they could do for me, but the shock of our abrupt separation left me confused and brokenhearted. I was suddenly and unexpectedly a lonely, down-and-out dog. Being abused by a loved one was horrible, but losing both home and family was absolutely terrifying.

To make matters worse, total strangers started looking me over, poking and prodding. I didn't know what was happening, and my cheerful, loving personality quickly disappeared. They de-wormed me and stuck me with needles. Then they topped it off by putting a chip in me so I couldn't even run away without being brought back to this scary place. I pulled away from them whenever I could, and they wrote on my chart: *Timid. Does not tolerate handling.* Can you imagine? Just a day earlier that description of me would have made no sense.

Let me tell you, it was really rough. I felt like I was going crazy—all those new smells, all those busy people rushing around, all those dogs barking and yelping. I've lived with cats, and call me weird if you like, I'm okay with them. But so many noisy, cooped-up dogs drove me bonkers. I started to panic, and my whole body trembled.

Even though I hated being there, I'm thankful now for those who watched over me. I didn't appreciate it at the time, but while I was at the shelter, I ate good meals and met wonderful people. Some of them didn't even get paid; they were there just because they love animals and want to help us. But all I could think about at the time was my own misery. The days and nights were excruciatingly long—and sad. I was used to running free and being part of the family fun. Now I was imprisoned and unloved. That first week seemed more like a century.

It was June, such a pretty time of year. But here I was, unfairly punished, hopelessly trapped, and downright distraught. *Why is this happening to me? Could this be my fault?* I didn't know what to do, so I started nervously chomping on my leg, and it started to bleed.

Fortunately, things took a turn for the better when the New Hope people came to look us over. These are people from various rescue groups who give animals like me a new start. If they can see the slightest glimmer of hope for finding us good homes, they'll even snatch us away from "death row." (*I still shudder at the thought!*)

The people from Rawhide Rescue in nearby New Jersey took a special liking to me. They overlooked the graying chin that others found so discouraging and looked right into my heart. They wasted no time in getting me out of the shelter, to a place where I'd get more of what I needed and craved: a little extra TLC and the assurance that I wouldn't be put down. I got to live in one of their foster homes so I could relax and feel better about myself. Then they put me up at an animal hotel—they called it a kennel—while I waited for a new home.

Thanks to my friends at Rawhide Rescue, my inner light was rekindled and I began to trust again. Then my cheerful, loving disposition reappeared, and photos of me were posted on the Internet with descriptions that captured my true essence:

> *Jessie has tons of love and affection to give. She adores people of all sizes and loves to be showered with attention. Her personality is loving and gentle. She is attentive and walks nicely on a leash. If you're interested in a loyal companion who only wants to please you, Jessie is the one for you!*

But even though my new friends tried their hardest to help me feel better, I was still very upset. My life was filled with uncertainty—more new places and faces, more moving around, and more not knowing.

Won't my family ever come and get me? Can't they find a way to help the kid who hurt me, so we can all live together again? I had lots of questions, but no good answers.

I started to feel sick and kept sneezing all the time. They examined me and gave me some medicine, but instead of getting better, I only got worse. I couldn't even go to the adoption party at the pet store, because they were afraid I might make the other dogs sick. It was so depressing, like having a dark cloud hanging over me.

I could only lie there wondering how I'd ever get adopted if I couldn't go out and meet people. And that same pitiful question kept hounding me…

Will I ever stop hurting?

"Paws"
for Lessons Learned

Life's unfair, but don't despair. Look for the good.

Hang in there! There are a lot of nice people out there.

Accept help when it's needed. Then plan to pay it back and pass it on many times over.

Bark up the Right Tree

CHAPTER 2

I Believe in Miracles!

Do you think God hears our cries and feels our pain? Can God turn sadness into joy and bring good out of a bad situation? All I can say is that God certainly worked a miracle in *my* life!

As I lay in the kennel whining and pining, something unusual was happening fifty miles away. A woman named Ruth was taking her early morning walk when, out of the blue, she envisioned a dog pulling a child in a wagon. This vision took root in her mind and heart, and it grew and grew every time she went for a walk.

She suspected that her vision was somehow related to a seemingly impossible dream she'd been contemplating for a long time. She had a wonderful dream of creating a development of small homes centered around a park-like common area. It would be a place where adoptive families and rescued animals could love and support each other. This great big idea (*Ruth calls it Kids 'n' Kritters*) also includes a chapel, an amphitheater, childcare, health and veterinary care, and outreach programs—all run by volunteers.

Ruth wondered if the wagon-pulling dog might be a step toward making that dream come true. Maybe the dog could draw attention to animals in need of homes and also to children like the little girls she loved so much who lived in a nearby group home. Ruth could see the dog writing a book or two and perhaps even being a guest on the Oprah Show!

And no matter what exciting dog-related idea came into her mind, the dog's name was always Jessie. She wondered why, because she didn't know any people or animals by this name. But she could vividly imagine the dog being widely known and loved, raising funds for good causes, and giving young children buttons with a picture and slogan on them: *Jessie's pulling for you! Now, you pull for Jessie! Be the best you can be!*

When Ruth forced herself to think realistically about getting a dog, she found her heart being drawn upward and her inner spirit saying, "This can't be meant for now, Lord. I already have more to do than I can handle. And You know that even though hubby Hugo likes dogs, he doesn't want one. He's 78 years old, has never had a dog, and thinks that owning one would tie us down. Of course, *I* would love to have a dog. I haven't had one for 45 years, but I can wait!"

She immediately heard a Godly chuckle in her heart that replied, "You know what, Ruth? Hugo and a dog are not necessarily mutually exclusive—it's not just one or the other. Trust me, they can live together very happily. Hugo just doesn't realize the joy he's been missing."

When Ruth got over *that* shock, she dashed into action! To the Internet she went, looking for a strong dog named Jessie. She considered what kind of dog would enjoy pulling a wagon. She thought first of a Siberian husky because she recalled going on a dogsled ride in a New York City department store when she was a small child. Then she thought of a St. Bernard because her daughter was pulled in a cart by one of those gentle giants when *she* was a toddler.

Ruth knew that a St. Bernard would be much too big for her to handle, so she concentrated on the husky. To her amazement, she immediately found a Jessie listed on a husky adoption website. She sent a couple of e-mails to the organization but received no response. Meanwhile, she researched information on various breeds, and her heart was drawn toward the Labrador retrievers. They're easy-going and good with children, and certainly big and strong enough to pull a wagon.

Ruth decided to try Petfinder, a website that features homeless pets from thousands of adoption groups. Her quest for a dog named Jessie was made a whole lot easier when she found out she could search by the pets' names. She was surprised by the number of Jessies out there—fish, guinea pigs, cats, dogs, and even a horse. When she narrowed her search to *dogs* named Jessie, she still came up with a long list.

There were Jessies in California, Ohio, Florida, and New Hampshire that looked like good possibilities. But Ruth lived in New Jersey. She inquired about a few of them, not knowing how she'd ever get to them or they to her, but nothing fell into place. She began to get discouraged when she thought of all the roadblocks piling up in front of her. She also knew it would be a big challenge to get this idea past Hugo, so she seriously considered giving up on her search for this elusive mystery dog.

Ruth's heart spoke to God once again. "I've done all I can, Lord, so it seems to me that You must have this slated for another time and place, right?"

No Godly chuckle *this* time, just total silence.

"Okay," Ruth sighed. "I'll look just one more time."

And guess what! That's when she saw *me*! Right at the top of the list: *A 7-year-old, medium-sized Labrador retriever mix named Jessie.* I looked adorable in the photos, of course. In fact, I reminded Ruth of Tony, her favorite neighborhood dog. She didn't know why she had missed me in her previous searches; either my entry had just been posted, or she had skipped over it because I was already seven years old.

"But hey!" Ruth thought, "I'm 63, and Jessie's only 49 in people years. It sounds pretty good to me!" And her heart skipped a beat when she saw that this great-looking dog (*said in all modesty, of course*) was in New Jersey. Just an hour away!

After reading what they wrote about me, Ruth knew that we were being brought together for a very special reason. She also knew, without a doubt, that I was the Jessie God had in mind all along.

And that, my friends, is why I say …

I believe in miracles!

"Paws"
for Lessons Learned

Think big. It's so much fun and brings such big rewards.

Take a chance and step out in faith. A miracle may be brewing.

Follow your heart. The best is waiting for you—especially if you're thinking of others.

Bark up the Right Tree

CHAPTER 3

Finding a Way

Petfinder invites people to e-mail the pets they would like to adopt. So, the first thing Ruth did was e-mail me to see if I'd enjoy visiting nursing homes, pulling a wagon, letting children read to me, helping with fundraisers, and getting involved in new activities. She also told me about herself and her family.

Ruth taught third grade for nine years. She married Hugo, and after their daughter, Elisa, was born, she worked in Hugo's international business. Ruth and Hugo are now semi-retired and enjoy writing and using the Internet. Elisa is all grown up and works as a specialist helping challenged adults. She has a little baldy ("peach-fuzz") Sphynx cat named Annabelle who actually likes dogs. Can you believe that?!

Ruth assured me in her e-mail that my being older, like Hugo and her, meant that we'd all take it easy and do only what we enjoy. She promised lots of walking, a nice soft bed, a room of my own near the sliding back door, and plenty of toys to play with. My friend Denise at Rawhide Rescue wrote back to Ruth on my behalf to let her know that she was sure I'd be very interested (*a definite understatement*). Ruth then filled out an adoption application and was invited to meet me at a pet store adoption day.

Ruth was hoping to find a way to get Hugo as excited about me as she was so they could go to the adoption day together. Fat chance! But knowing that God specializes in the impossible, she started using her walking time to make a plan.

She couldn't simply approach Hugo and try to explain all this. He needed a little softening up first. A nicely-prepared letter would work well. At least it worked well years earlier when Ruth wanted to take in a foster child. This time she'd make the letter humorous. She'd tell him some shocking and ridiculously exaggerated bad news so that her plan to adopt me would then seem like good news.

Ruth put together a really imaginative letter. First she wrote about some startling bad news: their life savings were gone, her eyesight was failing, and she planned to run away with a younger man. Then she quickly admitted that she was just kidding and wrote about the good news—me!

She described how I'd get her out of bed early, add a sparkle to the household, keep the focus on enjoying today, and chase the squirrels out of the attic in the winter. She also talked about me eventually writing a book—she knew he'd like that. She ended the letter by saying:

I know we're busy, but this needn't be the straw that breaks the camel's back. It can be the straw that strengthens it! Let's go for it, with positive expectations and a song in our hearts! Whaddaya say?

Ruth planned to give Hugo the letter on the morning of the adoption day so he could think about it while she and Elisa went shopping. But while Ruth was on an early morning errand, Lisa from Rawhide Rescue called to tell her that I couldn't attend the adoption day because I was sick.

The problem with this courteous phone call was that Hugo answered the phone. At first he thought Lisa was selling something, so he told her to take him off the call list! Of course Lisa explained who she was and told him about me. When Ruth came home, Hugo immediately asked, "Why are you talking to people about getting a dog?"

Ruth froze. She couldn't believe that he had somehow found out about me before getting her letter. "Why do you ask?" she replied.

Hugo gave her the message from Lisa, and Ruth quickly handed him the letter she'd prepared. Without saying a word, she grabbed Elisa and rushed out to go shopping. Obviously, the plan was falling apart.

Hugo was ready to talk when Ruth returned home. He was still a bit shaken, though, because when he first opened Ruth's letter, his eyes fell on the part about her eyesight failing. This hit him like a bolt of lightning, and he figured that Ruth was probably looking for a seeing-eye dog. (*Wow! That wasn't supposed to happen.*) Only when he read the entire letter did he realize that it was meant to be funny. I guess that's what happens when people know you'd never lie to them.

Ruth apologized profusely for upsetting him. Then she told him the whole story—how she found me, why she wrote the letter, her plans for me—and made it clear that if he didn't agree with adopting me, she would understand.

Ruth rarely asks for much, but when she does, it's really big! And because Hugo loves Ruth and enjoys seeing her enthusiastic and happy, it's hard for him to say no. So, he reacted to the idea of adopting me the same way he'd reacted to welcoming the foster child, the Fresh Air Fund children, the exchange student…

He said, "Yes!"

Ruth hugged him and thanked him and promised, "This will be a blessing for you, too. Just wait and see!"

Things were now looking mighty good for me, even though I didn't know it yet. I was still a sad and lonely pooch trying to make the most of a devastating situation. I hated being sick and wondered how much longer I could go on like this.

"Paws"
for Lessons Learned

Avoid the type of kidding that can hurt others. It hurts you, too.

Be willing to work hard to get what you want.

Consider others when making decisions.

Bark up the Right Tree

CHAPTER 4

Here I Come!

While Ruth was busy persuading Hugo, I was still stuck at the kennel. The medicine they gave me still wasn't working. I got worse, not better. What I needed was a loving home, which is by far the *best* medicine!

Little did I know that things were already moving in that direction. All that remained to be done in the adoption process was the home-check. Ruth didn't even come and meet me first. As far as she was concerned, I was already her dog. And if all went well with the home-check, I'd have a loving home to call my own.

My friend Denise accompanied me on the home-check. But first, she gave me a bath so I'd be presentable to my potential family. As we traveled to Ruth's house, I wondered what was happening. *Am I finally going back to my family? Or will this just be another new place with more things to upset me? Or could this end up being the death of me?*

Thankfully, it was "none of the above." Instead, I was on my way to the adventure of a lifetime—becoming part of a brand new family.

My new family members tingled with excitement as the doorbell rang. Ruth's hand visibly trembled with anticipation as she slowly opened the door. And then, the magic moment! We met each other face-to-face for the very first time.

While they were treasuring the moment, I barreled my way into the house and began to explore. I went right to my downstairs bedroom where I found a bone-shaped prize to chew on. I clamped my teeth around it and wouldn't release it, not even when Denise tried to show off how obedient I am. But despite my rude behavior, I was welcomed with open arms.

"How beautiful you are!" they said admiringly, "and so *big*!" At over 70 pounds, I guess I was a surprisingly large "medium-sized" dog. It was mostly solid muscle, of course—with perhaps a wee bit of flab due to my recent inactivity.

We all went out onto the back patio and visited for awhile, chatting and getting to know each other. Ruth put a bandana around my neck, and I beamed from head to tail! I flashed a big doggie smile, the kind that even people can recognize. And Hugo captured the moment for posterity with his little digital camera.

I delighted no end in all that heart-warming attention. But one of us, Annabelle the cat, seemed to be somewhat lacking in enthusiasm. I guess she saw me as an oversized intruder.

But she still stuck close and kept an inquisitive eye on me. You know how it is with cats and curiosity!

Denise gave Ruth my medicine and some good information about owning a dog. She instructed Ruth that if things didn't go well, for any reason, she was not to bring me to a shelter. I had to be returned to Rawhide Rescue, because the people there would never give up trying to find the best home for me. Ruth understood and readily agreed to this wonderfully compassionate rule. But she knew down deep in her heart that she would never give me up.

Finally, Denise was ready to leave—but I got to stay! I ran right upstairs to tour the rest of my new home. The windows were low enough for me to just walk over and look out. There were even windows in the roof to brighten the room. Comfy carpets here and there, and a terrace out back with a river and woods in full view. Obviously the amenities were great, but what I liked most was the warmth and love that surrounded me from the second I arrived. What a wonderful new beginning it was for all of us—Ruth, Hugo, Elisa, Annabelle the cat, and me.

Yes, indeed, I was being given a marvelous chance at a brand new life. And that's nothing to sneeze at. But I sneezed anyway (*again and again*) because of my respiratory infection. And with each sneeze, thick mucus flew in all directions. I was so embarrassed, but Ruth just wiped my nose and cleaned the mess off the floor, wall, appliance, or whatever. She made me feel right at home—*my* home!

She showed me my food and water bowls, raised above the ground just enough to make it easy for a tall dog like me to reach. She also showed me the special bed they'd purchased for me and the bulletin board in my room that said, "Jessie's Place"—ideal for displaying photos, certificates, and articles related to my new life.

I now had everything any dog could desire, and for the first time in what seemed like an eternity, I could relax and enjoy my home, my people, my place in the world. I felt so grateful and showed it with lots of wags and kisses. Here I was, once again part of an active family, ready to share in all the ups and downs of life with people who love and care for me. If I could have spoken out loud, I would have shouted, "Hot diggity dog!"

Good-bye to the kennel and the helpless, hopeless feeling that was threatening to take me down. Hello to my new home and all those special missions that are calling my name.

Ready or not...

Here I come!

"Paws"
for Lessons Learned

Let go of the past; make good use of today!

Go with the flow; roll with life's punches.

Look to the future and say to yourself, "It'll get greater, later!"

Bark up the Right Tree

CHAPTER 5

Patience, Please!

Those first days, weeks, and months of any new relationship are generally referred to as the honeymoon period. That time can also be a shocking dose of reality. For us, it was definitely a give-and-take, forget-the-fantasies experience. I admit it! I was still pretty scared and extremely cautious. I think my new family was, too. But we all survived (*and, dare I say, enjoyed*) this get-acquainted time. Our secret? Lots of patience and understanding.

For example, I hated the chip-filled bed they'd purchased for me and avoided it like the plague. Hugo and Ruth caught on quickly and returned it without comment. Then they foolishly went out and bought me another bed. This time it was a squishy one that puffed up all around me when I sat down. Of course I hated that one, too, and showed it by lying on the hardwood floor next to it. Finally, they got wise and washed up a scruffy old quilted bedcover. I loved it! They folded it a couple of times and set it out for me. I jumped right into it! (*Ahh! This is home!*)

I also let them know right away that I preferred *not* to have my own bedroom. The last thing I wanted was to be shut off by myself at night—on a different level of the house, no less. I know they were trying to be nice and give me my space, but they needed to understand that I just wanted to be with the family. One night in my room downstairs more than convinced me. There had to be a better alternative.

I knew that the master bedroom was off-limits, so I went for the next best thing—Elisa's room. Her bedroom was right across from the master bedroom, and she and Annabelle needed another roommate. So, I cried a bit at bedtime and turned on the charm when Elisa tried to soothe me. Sure enough, she melted. Starting on night two, she slept as usual in her bed, and I slept in my bed on the floor next to her. And Annabelle? She slept wherever she wanted to, of course!

My daily walks were another challenge. Ruth had wanted a pulling dog, but I guess I was more than she bargained for. You might even say *I* walked her. Her hands hurt from holding me back as we toured the neighborhood. Hugo and Elisa couldn't get me to slow down either. I think my enthusiasm was getting the best of me (and them, too!).

Elisa observed me carefully and declared, "I think Jessie is used to jogging." So, Ruth tried running a little with me—until we both started limping from too much of a good thing. So, we slowed our pace a bit, and I gradually started pulling less and less.

My upper respiratory infection was another problem we had to overcome little by little. I finished my pills, but I still wasn't well. Even if I had been perfectly healthy, I still would've had to go to the vet. The adoption process required a visit to the family veterinarian during the first month in my new home. But when Ruth called for an appointment, Dr. Garbaccio was on vacation. We tried to wait for his return, but one quiet evening, as I lay stretched out in the carpeted Florida Room (*the one with the glorious skylights*), I started making sudden, unexpected choking sounds. Ruth and Elisa, scared half to death, rushed me to the all-night emergency room at a nearby animal hospital.

When the vet began to examine me, I surprised everyone by snapping at him as he poked my rear underside. They thought I didn't like men, but I was just protecting myself from more abuse. As soon as I realized he was trying to help me, I let him give me a chest x-ray. I was even grateful that he suggested I wear a harness instead of my collar for the time being. We left the hospital with new meds and happy hearts, celebrating the fact that I didn't have to stay there overnight.

Once again, Elisa was quick to notice that I had a problem with people touching my ears and tail area. I think her work with special-needs people has made her a very sensitive and caring person—or perhaps those qualities led her to that career. Either way, she saw right into my heart and instinctively knew that I was still suffering from the scars of my abuse. But, thanks to the kindness and gentleness I consistently received from my new family, my ear and tail issues gradually faded away and my trust in people steadily increased.

I became so trusting that I eventually let Ruth "furminate" my tail as well as my body. I came with lots of loose fur, both on me and flying off me—another unexpected surprise for my new owners, no doubt. Denise from Rawhide Rescue explained that my winter coat may not have been fully brushed out, so Ruth got something called a Furminator®. It's a nice little comb-like gadget that gets most of the excess fur out. Even dogs that hate to be brushed seem to like it, but I didn't need much persuading. I absolutely love to be brushed. In fact, I even love to be vacuumed!

When Dr. Garbaccio later returned from his vacation, we scheduled my official checkup. I was feeling much better by then and fully expected to get a clean bill of health. Dr. G. lifted me right up and put me on the table to be weighed and inspected. He then told Ruth I could easily afford to lose a couple of pounds. That was a bit of a disappointment, since I sure do love my treats!

The good doctor also told Ruth that it's quite normal to take eight weeks to completely recover from an infection like the one I had. It can take even longer, he said, for me to get fully acclimated to my new life and for my true self to be fully revealed. He felt strongly, however, that I'd do very well, and he complimented Ruth for adopting me so late in my life.

As it turns out, it was even later than my new family expected. My original family told the shelter I was seven years old, but according to Dr. G., the cataracts starting to form on my eyes, the condition of my teeth, and other indicators put me closer to ten years of age. Of course I know exactly how old I am, but like most gals my age, I'm not telling. I'm in great shape and enjoying life, so who cares about a silly number!

Age certainly had nothing to do with what Hugo felt was my lack of interest in playing. He loves a little nonsense, you know, and he's quite a mischief-maker! So he was disappointed that I didn't seem to be the playful dog described in my Internet dossier. He was baffled when I didn't enjoy balls, sticks, and Frisbees® or respond to his playful advances.

But all I needed was the right toy. And once again, it was Elisa who came to the rescue. She bought me a squeaky rubber bone, and the puppy in me immediately came out in full force. To this day, it remains the only type of toy I enjoy playing with. It's colorful and feels really good in my mouth—and I love the squeak! If someone accidentally (or purposely) steps on it, I come running to claim it. What fun I have growling playfully when someone tries to take the bone from my mouth. My tail wags with joy when people chase me to get it, and I welcome all our guests by greeting them, toy-in-mouth!

I now have a whole collection of squeaky rubber bones in a variety of colors. Some have lost their squeak because they've been played with so much, but they're still in the game because I can hear the air escaping when they're stepped on.

I proudly line up my armada of squeak-bones as I sit at my lookout post in the dining room, a great place to watch out for adversaries approaching from any direction—the kitchen, the Florida Room, or the living room. The greatest fun is when Hugo and I tease each other. He frantically tries to steal one bone after another, in very shrewd and tricky ways. While I'm busy trying to take back the bone he's stepping on, he's already stepping on another one to divert my attention. I run from one bone to the next, growling as he tries to grab them away from me.

It may sound like I'm bragging, but sometimes the only way to protect my bones from thieves like him is to hold on to all of them at once. Believe it or not, I've been seen trotting around our house with all five of them in my mouth and sporting a bit of attitude that says …

I dare you to take one!

"Paws"
for Lessons Learned

Take care of, and enjoy, those you love.

Be flexible—make accommodations for others' interests and needs.

Look for (and bring out) the best in each other.

Bark up the Right Tree

CHAPTER 6

It's a Two-Way Street

I can't begin to count the ways in which my loved ones have gently and patiently helped me to heal my wounds. They embraced, empowered, and encouraged me. They allowed me to be myself, to feel comfortable in my own fur.

They skillfully redirected my attention when I continued to chew on that open sore on my leg—and before long, it was gone and forgotten. They also coached me on how to take it easy when lying down on the hardwood floor. No more plopping down with a loud *clunk*, a habit that gave me those hardened calluses on both of my elbows.

How relieved I was when they understood that I didn't enjoy the doggie play areas that some of the parks provide. All those rambunctious dogs in one place overwhelm me and remind me of my days at the shelter.

I also appreciated that they didn't make me suffer the indignity of being thrown into the water to literally sink or swim. I know they were surprised that, despite my webbed paws and aquatic retriever heritage, I had no interest in frolicking in the nearby dog-friendly lake. Other dogs jumped in exuberantly, carrying back the sticks thrown in by their laughing owners. But me? I tiptoed gingerly along the water's edge, glad for any excuse to leave and explore the mountain paths instead. I might venture a step or two into the water, but if I never get to swim it's okay with me (*and* with them).

As you can see, my family has been very kind and considerate. But it's been a two-way street. I've also gotten to exercise *my* "patience muscles" with *them*.

I've learned to patiently put up with things that are a little silly and maybe even a little embarrassing. The prime example is that I now have a middle name. How many non-pedigreed dogs have *that*? I must admit it's a lovely name—Grace (Ruth's mom's name, Elisa's middle name, and in the title of our charitable foundation). Believe it or not, it was Hugo's idea!

I also ♪*let her call me Sweetheart.*♪ Why not? I'm the only one on whom Ruth bestows that dubious honor, so I may as well enjoy it. And I don't even mind when Ruth and Hugo refer to each other as "Mother" or "Daddy" when talking to me. Why, I even jump to attention when Ruth gets annoyed and calls me *Jessie Grace*!

I'm also the proud owner (*ha*!) of a bright red raincoat with an ear-covering hood, which I always shake off because I like to have my ears free. I also have what Ruth calls a "cutely-decorated" winter jacket. And if Ruth ever locates a doggie sweater *she* likes, I'm sure that it, too, will be a part of my somewhat frivolous wardrobe.

Sometimes I feel like saying, "Give me a break!" But then I decide to go along with it and lovingly humor them. And you know what? It actually feels pretty good to be "humanized," because it shows me over and over again that I am indeed part of the family. Even wearing a witch's hat to go trick-or-treating on Halloween can have its good points!

Getting used to riding in the car with the doggie seat belt took the most patience, but it was a serious necessity. My flopping around at every turn put us, and others, in danger. Whenever we go somewhere by car, I now get buckled into the car-harness, like a horse being saddled. Ruth especially enjoys this because she always wanted a horse, so I'm a little like the horse she never had. Once I'm harnessed, I jump into the blanket-covered backseat and get hooked onto the center seat belt. Then we can hit the road!

I get a nice view from all sides in the little Mazda Protégé, now considered to be "Jessie's car." Sounds like I'm a really spoiled dog with my own car, doesn't it? Of course, I'm not easily fooled. I know that they want to limit my mess and doggie smell to the older, smaller car. Not that I'm complaining, mind you. I love to ride in the car, and I scramble like crazy to get into my harness.

But getting re-harnessed to return home after a fun walk is another story. I purposely keep moving around, feigning interest elsewhere, as Ruth tries to get the harness over my head. I then refuse to jump into the car until they entice me with a little treat. I have them pretty well trained, don't I?

Don't get me wrong. I do my part whenever I can—like when I'm told to "Put it down!" if I try to leave the house with one of my squeak-bones. Granted, whenever I do manage to sneak one outside, I drop it while searching for the ideal place to relieve myself—and promptly forget about it. Still, it irks me each time I have to relinquish it at the door. But seeing their delight when I obediently drop the toy is fun, too. And, after all, it's the least I can do for them.

I also acquiesce to a monthly shower. In the warm weather, it's a hoot being soaped up and hosed down in the backyard while playing with the high-flying water. In the cooler weather, however, we take this activity indoors—into the shower stall of the master bedroom. I'm normally not allowed in that bedroom, so when I'm told to enter, I either slink in reluctantly with my tail between my legs or I follow the trail of treats until I'm unexpectedly trapped in the master bathroom shower "cage." Ruth comes in with me, minimally dressed and wearing her beach sandals, ready for the upcoming challenge.

Being in this confined space makes me a little nervous, so Ruth calms me down with music and humor. She might sing a song or say something funny as we work up a lather. Like the time she told me about those ridiculous but memorable television commercials for Maidenform® undergarments. They aired when she was a teenager, and this particular ad campaign had dream themes like, *I dreamt I sailed the Nile…climbed the Himalayas…took an African safari…in my Maidenform "unmentionable."* Ruth jokingly says that *we* are now a "dream team" since she's dressed appropriately. Our theme, of course, would be *I dreamt I washed my dog…*

All in all, our bathing routine is a fairly quick and easy procedure thanks to Ruth's entertainment and the handheld shower nozzle that keeps the water close and not flying all over (*until I shake, of course, which makes it more like a nightmare than a dream*). The best part is the wonderful drying massage with fluffy towels and maybe some heavenly heat from Ruth's hair dryer. In any event, cleanliness is a requirement for visiting nursing homes and doing other service work, so I might as well get used to it.

Something else I'm good at is patiently waiting while Ruth and Hugo stop to chat with friends—right in the middle of a perfectly lovely walk. I generally end up lying down on the grass or asphalt, yawning away while they do their thing. I don't fuss and complain; I just let them chat to their hearts' content.

I also dutifully listen as Ruth practices her biblical storytelling by reciting her favorite Scriptures to me. This is good practice for when I'll let children read to me someday. The Scripture I like most says:

Love is patient and kind, never jealous, boastful, proud, or rude. It isn't selfish or quick-tempered; it doesn't keep a record of wrongs that others do. It rejoices in the truth…and is always supportive, loyal, hopeful, and trusting. Love never fails.

This is, indeed, the kind of love that my new family has lavished on me, and it has made all the difference in my life. On the other paw, *I* have added immeasurable joy to *their* lives, too. You should see the way we greet each other first thing in the morning or when they return after slipping out of the house for a few hours—or even for a few minutes! The wags, the hugs, the doggie kisses, the belly rubs, the baby talk, the sheer ecstasy. It doesn't get any better than this—at least not here on earth!

"Paws"
for Lessons Learned

Be patient with others, and appreciate patience extended your way.

Add an element of fun to every challenge—then it's easier to be patient!

Strive toward a well-balanced give-and-take.

Bark up the Right Tree

CHAPTER 7

New Friends, Both People and Pets

As I adjusted to life with my new family, I became healthier with each passing day. The fur that had dulled while I was so stressed out regained its shine, and my velvety coat became wavy again. Ruth took on the job of wiping the ooze from the inside corners of my eyes (*a motherly task that's never done*), and my teeth looked and felt so much better since Dr. G. removed some of the caked-on tartar. The monthly application of my vet-recommended flea and tick control did its job well without alienating friends or masking my signature essence-of-dog aroma. Indeed, I was more than ready to step out and become an active part of the exciting outside world.

Stepping out was fun because I was already a bit of a celebrity. Ruth had sent the local newspaper one of the photos that Hugo had taken of us on the day I arrived, and it appeared in the paper, in living color, along with an article all about me. I tried not to let the instant fame go to my head, but I couldn't help basking in it while it lasted. So I lapped it up when two of our town librarians left Hugo at the check-out desk while they quickly ran outside to make a fuss over me! I sure hope they'll be pleased when I present them with a complimentary copy of this book.

Ruth also started taking me to the First Dog Training Club, an obedience school where I met all kinds of new friends. Don't tell Ruth, but I think obedience school is more for the people than the dogs. Ruth didn't have a clue about how to hold the leash, how to talk to and encourage me as we walk, and all that good dog-owner stuff. Fortunately, my new friend Ward, a trainer at the club, helped us out. She gave both Ruth and me a little extra TLC, which we sorely needed and definitely appreciated.

Elisa also introduced me to some of her developmentally-challenged friends where she works. They loved me, and I, of course, loved them. One young man had experience with dogs, and when he said, "Sit!" I immediately sat—to the delight of all who watched. When I'm certified as a Canine Good Citizen and an International Therapy Dog, I hope I can visit with them more often and get to know them better.

I met still more people at our annual church picnic. It was held at a park, so I romped around in the great outdoors for hours, enjoying the picnickers—young, old, and in between—and the food, too, of course. I especially enjoyed Ruth's long-time buddy, Martha, who brought her wheelchair. I hung out with Martha for awhile and practiced being the dog in Ruth's vision by unintentionally giving her a little ride around the park—she kept holding my leash so she had no choice but to go with me!

I also had a blast with some of the girls from the Children's Aid and Family Services home. They came to the picnic and took to me like flies to honey and vice versa! We had a real kinship in knowing that we'd all been torn away from our original families. But they, unfortunately, are still waiting for the safe and happy homes they need and deserve. The good news is that they're living in a wonderful group home in the meantime.

Know what else I liked about the picnic? Ruth and her friend Betty, who were in charge of the games, made me an important part of one of the games. I got to show off a bit by guessing which hand held the treat. I'd jump up and touch a hand, and if it contained the treat, I got to eat it. If the treat wasn't there, the person got a point for that team. They called the game "Fool the Dog" or something like that, but they're the ones who got fooled. Even if I guessed incorrectly, I'd just jump up, touch the other hand, and get the treat anyway.

In addition to all my new people-friends, I've also been making animal-friends. Elisa's little Sphynx cat, Annabelle Leigh (another one blessed with a middle name), is my closest friend. We're quite a sight—a "monster" dog and a dainty little cat. We're animal equivalents of those tall and short comic strip characters from years ago, Mutt and Jeff. Maybe we should be called "Mutt" and "Diva."

Annabelle and I like to chase each other around the house, and then we relax together beneath the skylight. She rubs against me when I'm lying down, and I lick her with my big, soft tongue. Only when we're vying for attention or food will I push her away with my ample snout, or she'll use her famous paw-to-snout movement to put me in my place. She's one feisty little gal whose brain more than makes up for what she lacks in brawn.

Imagine, if you will, a typical lazy day with Ruth relaxing on the couch and me lying on the floor next to her. Annabelle all of a sudden appears and prepares to jump up so she'll be closer to Ruth than I am. I push her away. Now she circles around and jumps onto the back of the couch, suddenly descending onto Ruth from above. Ruth is surprised, then laughs and says, "It must be raining cats. I'm sure glad it's not raining cats and *dogs*." I can only sit there dumbfounded, outwitted once again by the *reigning* cat!

Annabelle is fun, but I've got lots of dog acquaintances, too, you know. My first canine encounter in my new neighborhood was with Luke, a dog who gets paid to chase geese off a golf course. He also listens while kids read to him. That's something I plan to do, too—listen to kids, not chase geese.

Then I met a couple of dogs on our street who gave Ruth and me quite a fright. We've since found out that they're more bark than bite, if you know what I mean. But we didn't know that then, and one day the brawny male came running toward us, barking up a storm. I guess the electric fence wasn't on, and he came right into the street as if he would attack us. Like most bullies, he ended up backing down and was no threat at all. Meanwhile, I was cowering behind Ruth, who was busy trying to cower behind me! Hugo later told Ruth that he was concerned that I might be too timid to ever defend myself. But I was about to show him a thing or two.

Our neighbors, Vinny and Cilia, own a black Lab named Tony and a beautiful honey-colored golden retriever named Madison. Ruth was anxious for me to meet Tony, who looks a lot like me. She was sure we'd be the best of friends. When we saw Vinny out walking with Tony and Madison one day, Ruth buckled me up, and out we went to greet them. I was a little intimidated by the two dogs sniffing me at the same time, but we were getting along quite well—for the moment.

Vinny invited us to see their fenced-in backyard, and then he invited us into their house to meet Cilia. They were very hospitable, offering me a treat and a drink from their doggie water dish. Things were going along splendidly until Cilia started petting me. I guess it was more than Madison could bear—a strange new dog in *her* house, eating and drinking *her* stuff, and now being petted by *her* mom. Madison suddenly went berserk and attacked me. Growls reverberated, fur flew…and I fought back! Hugo would have been proud of me.

Everyone froze in shock until Vinny shouted to Cilia, "Get the gun, get the gun!"

Ruth's mouth opened wide in stunned anticipation. "No, No!" she thought. "It's not *that* bad!" Then she breathed a sigh of relief and her mouth closed with a smile as Cilia brought out a *water* gun.

Vinny "shot" Madison a few times, and Madison released her hold. As quickly as it had started, the fight was over. Tony, obviously upset by the near riot, walked us out in his gentlemanly way to bid us adieu.

You know what? Maybe Ruth is right. Maybe Tony and I *will* become good friends someday.

"Paws"
for Lessons Learned

Make all types of friends. Enjoy the diversity!

Defend yourself when absolutely necessary, but choose the way of peace and forgiveness whenever possible. (P.S.—Madison and I are now getting along pretty well.)

Be content with who you are and respectful of others. It wards off a lot of conflict.

Bark up the Right Tree

CHAPTER 8

Twinkle Toes, on the Go!

Just as Dr. G. had said, I was slowly but surely coming into my own—for better or for worse, depending on the perspective. As my upper respiratory infection faded away, my keen sense of smell returned. This made my life much more interesting, but it also meant that I no longer walked docilely along with my people.

I'd now surprise them by making sudden turns and about-faces in order to pursue an unexpected scent. Patience would wear thin as I'd dillydally to savor those alluring smells beckoning from all the wrong places. I also became super fussy about where and when I'd do my "business." In fact, I loved the sniffing game so much that I learned how to apportion my liquid waste the way my male counterparts do.

Sadly, my renewed ability to sniff with the best of them had no effect on my aim. I'm still not very good at covering my excrement. As usual, I step away from it, rev up my back legs, kick up a storm, and try to bury the evidence. The problem is that the dirt, leaves, and debris that I instinctively kick up are more likely to fly in the face of my beloved than hit their intended target. (*Psst! We dogs really have a better aim, but since we know you'll soon be pooper-scooping anyway, why cover it? It's more fun to send the storm your way! Ha, ha! Just kidding, of course!*)

When it comes to walking, all I can say is, *It's the greatest!* Ruth and Hugo are both avid walkers, and so am I. So off we go in many different directions. Our most frequented destination is the nearby park where we enjoy a brisk jaunt around the "lake." The "lake" is actually a huge grass field used for baseball and soccer, with a playground named for Mr. Lake. It's a great place to meet all kinds of people and pets who also circle the field, either with us or against us. We meet them all, because we go first in one direction and then in the other. That's how I met Maggie.

Maggie is a beautiful liver-colored field spaniel. She's a sight to behold as she walks along proudly, her gorgeous body of hair bouncing and almost touching the ground with her every movement. Her person, Michael, took a real liking to me because he once had a black Lab named Holly. Ruth noticed that he and Maggie had a special leash that let her ebb and flow as they walked. When Ruth asked him about it, he explained that it's a retractable leash that gives Maggie a lot of leeway since it lengthens and shortens automatically as she walks. And guess what! The next day we met him again, and he gave us a gift that truly changed our lives—the wonderful, sturdy, retractable leash that he had used with Holly.

The new leash has given me plenty of freedom and extra exercise. I can now stop and sniff while Ruth and Hugo keep walking. I've gotten pretty good at gauging just how far apart we can get before I feel a friendly tug or (*God forbid*!) a sudden stop. What fun it is to let them walk past me while I sniff, then run to catch up with them—and even surpass them by some twenty feet. I can now go about twenty feet in any direction—back or forth, in or out, left or right, straight or diagonal. I don't walk anymore. I trot…I prance…I bounce…I dance!

Ruth, who already called me her miracle dog, now calls me her Lippizaner stallion, because I move with graceful elegance, executing a fancy little side step once in a while. Hugo agrees that my feet barely touch the ground as I float along in rhythmic ecstasy, delighting them as well as myself. There's a sparkle in my eye and a twinkle in my toes whenever I dance on my new leash. So it's no wonder that Ruth also calls me "Twinkle Toes."

We have to take care, however, when using the leash because cars, bikers, skaters, and even walkers may not see the slim cord that connects us. We soon learned to gradually retract the leash when we see people or traffic, locking into the first eighteen inches where there's a regular strap for holding me close. We have to be ever alert so that a sudden change of direction by me won't cause a problem. We also learned not to retract it when there's too much slack in the cord, or it whips up its own storm. It can also be a problem if the heavy handle is accidentally dropped when the leash is extended—because it then barrels toward me at quite a speed. But despite these drawbacks, it's been worth its weight in gold because of all the joy it's given us.

That retractable leash has come with us on excursions to Bear Mountain State Park, Van Saun County Park, Ramapo Reservation, Ringwood Manor, and other wonderful, dog-friendly places. We enjoy all sorts of rivers, ponds, hiking trails, and sometimes even doggie playgrounds—from the outside looking in, of course. The best of the best is when we find a place that's deserted and safe enough for me to walk or run around as free as the breeze.

Among my most treasured memories are when Elisa and I have gone to Piermont, New York—our personal favorite. We walk along the narrow peninsula all the way to the pier overlooking the Hudson River. Along the way we encounter dogs, dogs, and more dogs—and some people, too. Maybe even that friendly fisherman who gives out yummy dog biscuits. He makes me feel like I've won the grand prize, and my heart sings ♫B-I-N-G-O. Yes, Bingo is my name-o.♫

En route to all these marvelous places I get so excited I tend to get very restless and whine with anticipation—especially if I can't stick my nose out an open window. I guess it's like me asking again and again, *Are we there yet?* And of course I'm thrilled when we finally get to where we're going. I'm so happy I can hardly contain myself as the leash replaces my seatbelt and I burst out of the car, ready for anything and everything.

Obviously, I'm one very lucky dog, eager to enjoy and savor each and every moment of my wonderful new life.

Our favorite television preacher, Joel Osteen, says that God pays us back double for all our suffering—maybe even in *this* life. That must be what's happened to me, because my suffering has been replaced with more blessings than I can count. Just look at me now! I'm one extremely grateful "Twinkle Toes" who's very much on the go … and a firm believer that the best is yet to come.

"Paws"
for Lessons Learned

Explore interesting places near and far.

Use gifts responsibly and well. Be thankful for them.

Let others be a part of the things you enjoy. Happiness shared is happiness multiplied.

CHAPTER 9

Loved One Lost!

It was one of those crazy, hazy, lazy days of summer. Definitely a dog-day afternoon. It was much too hot to walk on the pavement, so Ruth and I decided to venture onto the path at the end of our street.

I love the path. It's wooded and runs along the river—a dog's paradise. We live in the suburbs, but that path brings us into the wilderness where we not only see the usual squirrels, rabbits, chipmunks, birds, and insects, but also deer, raccoons, possums, woodchucks, geese, and even snakes. The trail is at least a half-mile long and comes out in another town, near a big reservoir.

The path is a great place to unwind, cool down, follow my nose, and sing a song or two (♪*I love to go a'wandering...*♪). Our hearts fill with joy as we bask in the peaceful beauty we find there. We're like a puppy and a kid again, pretending to be explorers in the midst of a bold adventure. Ruth, being the practical one, brings along a big plastic bag to collect litter along the way, and I bring enough enthusiasm for the two of us!

During these forest walks I get good practice obeying the "Go around!" command. It's something I mastered as soon as my retractable leash started letting trees, signs, fire hydrants, rocks, and bushes get between us. In the woods it's really hard to stay together because I sniff my way over branches, around trees, and into foliage, and of course, I change direction as soon as a new scent catches my fancy. So there's always a good chance I'll end up getting caught in my own "web," with Ruth having to inch her way into the tangled maze to free me. But we don't mind. It's all part of the adventure.

Our walks aren't just fun and games, though. I take my squirrel-chasing responsibilities very seriously. I must say, I'm a pretty good chaser even though I haven't caught anything yet. Ruth is okay with that because she wants a chaser, not a catcher. In fact, she's very amused when I stand there looking up at a tree long after the squirrel has jumped into another tree and slipped away. She teases me and says, "Now I see how the phrase 'barking up the wrong tree' came about!"

On this particularly sweltering day, our hike was following a predictable pattern. I chased some squirrels, barked up a few wrong trees, and then shifted my attention toward my favorite "game"—chipmunks! I raised my ears and lifted my front paw to help me concentrate. Then I pointed in the direction of the sound and movement. I was soon in my favorite position—behind up, tail wagging, and nose out of sight, searching beneath a rock, in a hole, or through a log.

While I was busy challenging the chipmunks, Ruth saw something move on the path ahead of us. We often see deer (*Sure wish Ruth would let me chase them!*), but this animal was too small to be a deer. It was more the size of a large rabbit. It noticed us and moved farther down the path. Then Ruth knew for sure it wasn't a rabbit. It didn't hop; it ran more like a little pig.

Ruth could see the mystery animal still ahead of us when I came bounding back onto the path. At that point, I had a very dirty nose and, as usual, no chipmunk. We continued down the path together and got steadily closer to the yet-to-be-identified animal. Then I got a quick glimpse of it, too.

But once again, the little creature ran on ahead. We noticed that it kept us in its sight, which was good because that meant we could also keep our eyes on *it*. We decided to stop and just wait a while before approaching it again. Then we walked ever-so-slowly toward it. This time it let us get closer and closer until…

All of a sudden it bolted and ran like crazy—right *toward* us! Imagine our surprise when we realized that this was no wild animal at all; it was a cute little Schnauzer pup! He looked well cared for, with his tail cut short and his whiskers long. But he was damp, matted, and messy, probably from running around in the woods—no doubt frightened and looking for the people who'd put that nice collar on him.

The adorable little fur-ball came right up to me. A lot of dogs, and people, seem to take an immediate liking to me. I guess it's because I have a mellow temperament and look friendly. But this little guy was awfully young and playful and wouldn't leave me alone. He was much too active for me, but I tried to be patient because I knew he was just a little lost dog in need of a friend.

He let Ruth try to pet him as he bounced up and down like a little rubber ball. But just like me, she didn't quite know what to do with him. Then we came up with a plan to get our new friend to safety. Actually Ruth thought of it, but I caught on right away. We'd put my leash on *him* and lead him home with us. It meant we'd have to cut our journey short and head back, but I didn't mind. In fact, I loved every step of the way, because I got to walk without a leash and doubly enjoy this wonderful adventure.

When we finally stepped out of the woods and onto our street, we passed a neighbor and showed off our new little friend as we headed to our back patio. Ruth called the police in our town and also in the town at the other end of the path, but no one had called in about a missing dog. They offered to take him to a shelter, but we thought it would be better if we could keep him for awhile, giving the owners a chance to call in looking for him.

The word *shelter* brought to mind some painful memories, so I was hoping this little fella wouldn't have to go there. Ruth said she was sure that our friends at Rawhide Rescue could easily find a good home for him, if necessary. He was so cuddly and full of fun, so easy to love.

But we certainly had to clean him up. So Ruth gave him her well-known "soap 'em up, hose 'em down, and towel 'em dry" routine. I shared my food and water with him. He was so hungry he gobbled up all the food, not even caring that some of it got on his long whiskers. He was such a happy little guy, glad to be safe and secure once again.

And all's well that ends well. In fact, this is one "dog-gone" story with a doggone happy ending. Soon, the telephone rang. Ruth answered and a young man said, "The police tell me that you have a little dog."

Before long, a van with a father, mother, and three children pulled up in front of our house. They had described our little puppy accurately, so we felt confident that he was theirs. And when they saw each other, we had no doubts.

The oldest child had tears in her eyes as she ran and scooped up her little lost-and-found doggie, hugging him tightly. They had suffered a great deal while he was missing, but now they were relieved and grateful. They kept saying, "Thank you. Thank you *so* much."

Ruth chatted with them and found out that they originally came from Mexico. They were new to the area; that's probably why the poor little pup couldn't find his way home.

And how did my new little friend react to being reunited with his family? He was obviously elated to be heading home in the arms of a loved one. But all of a sudden, he looked my way and started straining to get back to me! Everyone laughed because in his own way, he, too, was saying, "Thank you. Thank you so much. And, by the way, can I come back and play with you again sometime?"

I'd only known the little guy for an hour or two, and already I had a special place in my heart reserved just for him.

"Paws"
for Lessons Learned

Be on the lookout! Life is full of unexpected adventures.

Lend a helping paw whenever possible. It sure feels good, doesn't it?

Take care of our natural paradises so future generations of people and animals can also enjoy them.

Bark up the Right Tree

CHAPTER 10

Sidelined!

Sometimes we think we're invincible, don't we? We forget that we're only canine (*or human*) and get careless, throw caution to the wind, or just plain don't think. And once in a while things just happen through no fault of our own.

Ruth is still not sure what happened that morning when I went out the back of our house to do my business and returned limping. Could it be that I ran around our backyard, pretending to be Lassie on a life-saving errand, jumping over the low patio walls, making sudden turns, and maybe even slipping down the rugged slope to the river below us?

It's possible, but not probable. More likely, I was sniffing out a chipmunk by the riverbank and lost my footing. But regardless of the cause, the challenge was now a formidable one—getting around on three feet. Jumping into the car to go to the vet was a hassle, and just getting to the car was a problem because of the stairs in our bi-level home. It was quite an undertaking, but working together, we finally got there.

The diagnosis was quite somber. Dr. G. explained that I tore the ligament in my hind knee, a common injury for dogs, tennis players, and basketball players. It's caused by overextending the ligament when landing in a stressful or unnatural way.

He told us that veterinarians used to perform sophisticated surgery in such cases. A hole would be drilled into the dog's knee and then filled with grafted material from another part of the knee. But, due to his research and experience, Dr. G. now recommends rest, time, and glucosamine chondroitin supplements. This, he finds, works just as well, costs much less, and spares the dog quite a bit of discomfort.

He said I'd soon be up and around, but for the moment, I was a slightly overweight, 75-pound dog living in a home with two flights of stairs. The carpeted steps weren't too difficult to navigate, but the hardwood stairs leading down to the front door were now much too slippery for me. Hugo and Ruth rushed right out to get carpet treads. This made going down a lot easier, but I still had trouble climbing back up. Dr. G. told us to try using a towel as a lower-body sling to help carry my hind half up the stairs, but that turned out to be even more hazardous for me. (*Thanks, but no thanks, Mom and Dad—I'll somehow get up on my own!*)

Poor Ruth. She was so concerned and felt so sorry for me. She always kids that she's like a new mother, calling the doctor at the drop of a hat: "Jessie just ate something (or did something) I'm a little worried about. Should I bring her in?" (*He generally says, "No, just watch her carefully, and call if there's a problem."*) She even called him to ask about buying me a coat or sweater. Believe it not, he said, "Go ahead," because it gets mighty blustery in the winter, and the extra warmth is good for an older dog taking long walks.

I shouldn't make fun of Ruth for taking my welfare so seriously. After all, it's great that she reads all the latest dog books and keeps learning new things from the doggie websites that e-mail her. And I'm glad she takes Dr. G.'s advice and coats my supplement capsules with cream cheese before hiding them in my food, like a prize in a Cracker Jack® box. The trick works very well, especially because I love to eat the prize!

Dr. G. insisted that I take it easy to give my leg time to heal. He prescribed one month of caution and three months of the supplements. Mom pampered me by setting up a super-comfy inflatable mattress on the lower level, where I can get in and out without having to contend with the stairs. She added cozy blankets and brought down my feeding tray. She even joined me for awhile, talking and singing with me, just as she had done when Elisa was small and sidelined for a day or two.

After she left, the time passed slowly and boredom quickly set in. I tried not to feel sorry for myself. After all, sometimes we have to adjust to life and not the other way around. But I sure hated doing nothing all by myself.

I started to consider the beneficial side of a forced time-out. It can be a time of awareness and introspection, a chance to see things from a broader, more compassionate perspective, and an opportunity to philosophize, plan, and count the many blessings we take for granted.

So, I started thinking…

Funny, isn't it, that Elisa also has a friend named Tony, just like I do?

I'm so glad that Rebecca, a child who was without a home of her own, got adopted, too. She lives nearby, so we see her once in a while. She loves animals, especially the horse she's learned to ride, her two fun-filled ferrets, and me!

What would my friend Artie say about me now? He calls me "Moose" because he thinks I'm so big and strong. Now I'm sidelined like a wounded soldier. But I think Artie would understand. He's a Vietnam veteran who helps with house-cleaning every other week. He's always singing, humming, or whistling. He says it's better than thinking sad thoughts. He has a big dog named Jett and always brings me a couple of his huge dog biscuits—one for "hello" and one for "good-bye." I guess you can say that I'm glad to see him come, and I'm glad to see him go!

I'm proud of Ruth. She follows the advice of that song she learned in elementary school: ♪Make new friends but keep the old; the first are silver and the others gold.♪ *She keeps in touch with all sorts of people. She even wrote a letter to my former owners via that Staten Island shelter. She thought my family of the past would be glad to know that I'm doing so well, and she was hoping to learn more about my previous life. Too bad they haven't responded yet.*

Isn't it odd that so many dogs have people-names? In addition to Tony, Madison, and Maggie, there's Charlie across the street and Rosie around the corner. Go around another corner and there's Clyde and Keili, an energetic friend with a fancy Hawaiian name. We met Amy and Cindy at a park one day and enjoyed a wonderful stroll together, but for the life of me, I can't remember whether Amy was the dog or the person. And that cute little dachshund on the next street? We don't know his name, but I wouldn't be surprised if it's Tom, Dick, or Harry!

Imagine…just five months ago I was stuck in a shelter. Now I'm stuck here on this bed. But what a difference the circumstances make. I feel loved this time rather than abandoned.

I've forgiven those who disappointed and hurt me. That's why I'm so happy now. I wish everyone could forgive and forget so they could be happy, too.

How long will it be, Lord, until I can do all the exciting things You have in store for me?

After a while, my thoughts began to revitalize me, and I said to myself, "Enough is enough! I can do this!"

Without further ado, I got right up and climbed the two sets of steps on my own! I may not be able to run and greet people as usual, but they'll certainly hear my gaily-thumping tail against the hardwood floor.

It may be a while before I'm ready for another family hug—when I stand upright to join Ruth and Hugo in a loving embrace—and that's okay. I'm exactly where I want to be, on the upper level with my loving family. This is where the action is. This is where I'll make my speediest recovery and where I'll start to hop-to-it once again!

"Paws"
for Lessons Learned

Use your downtime creatively. It can revitalize your spirit.

Count your blessings every day. Don't take them for granted.

Be grateful for challenges. The bumpy road teaches us more, and demands more of us, than the smooth road does.

Bark up the Right Tree

CHAPTER 11

Wait for the Wagon

She's at it again! Ruth is singin' away. This time it's an old song from her childhood days. She says it just came to mind because it fit the occasion perfectly. The words go something like this:

♬ *Wait for the wagon, wait for the wagon,*

Wait for the wagon, and we'll all take a ride!

It's early Sunday morning, Miss Bessie by my side.

Let's all get together, and we'll all take a ride. ♬

It is, indeed, an appropriate song because we're still waiting for my wagon—the one I expect to pull someday soon. We can easily replace "Miss Bessie" with "Miss Jessie," can't we? And just like the song says, we're all waiting. Even if it arrives, we don't know when, or even *if*, I'll be ready and able to pull a child in it. I did get back on my four feet again after only a day or two of hopping around on three legs. But I still have to be extremely careful. I might look and feel great again, but my hind leg remains vulnerable for at least three months.

Fortunately, the timing's been good. The winter months lessened my desire and my opportunity to go outside. With Ruth and Hugo in Florida for their annual two-week vacation, Elisa took me on my walks. She uses the old-fashioned six-foot leash, so my trotting, prancing, bouncing, and dancing were curtailed. That's just what the doctor ordered.

Ruth wants to be sure I'm in tip-top shape before starting my pulling project. I sure hope I get to do it. I'm looking forward to pulling the kiddies—and maybe even getting a ride or two myself once in a while. It's true that I'm an older dog (*"senior citizen," as they say*), but I'm also tough and have lots of youthful enthusiasm. I expect that once my leg is healed, it will be even stronger than before.

Ruth did some Internet research on dogs pulling wagons, carts, and buggies and found that dogs can pull up to three times their weight. For me, that would be over 200 pounds! Certainly a 50-pound child shouldn't be a problem.

One day, we met a dog pulling his owner along the gravel path next to the Hudson River. He was pulling a two-wheeled cart, similar to the ones pulled by the trotting horses. The dog and woman looked like they were having such a great time, we just had to stop and talk with them. It turned out that this dog is super energetic and just loves to pull the woman around. What fun!

Of course, this isn't what Ruth has in mind. She leans more toward my pulling a little kiddie wagon that would be attractive to the children and give them a comfortable, secure feeling. She found lots of these on the Internet and even a kit that would replace the wagon's movable handle with a specially-made shaft and dog harness. But, for the time being, she's not going to purchase anything.

Instead, she prays about it and always keeps her spiritual antennae out to see what feedback the Lord might provide. She did tell her friend Marge, the garage sale guru, to be on the look-out for a wagon. She also sent a photo of us to the local paper with an article entitled "Wanted: The Perfect Waggin' Wagon." The article appeared in the newspaper, but so far, no wagon has materialized. Meanwhile, Ruth just contentedly sings, ♪*We'll wait for the wagon, and we'll see what's in store!*♪

"If God wants us to have a wagon," she says, "one will come our way. If not, that's okay, too."

And it's good we did wait, because (*You won't believe this!*) after one month of easy-does-it living and almost three months of continued glucosamine chrondroitin supplementation, I hurt the same leg again. We're not sure how it happened, but the vet said I probably had a bad landing again. I do recall jumping onto the driveway from the nearby wall before Ruth could stop me. I was in mid-air when she yelled, "Stop!"

Whatever the cause of the injury, we found ourselves right back at square one. Only this time, my three healthy legs—and my spirit—were stronger. I even insisted on leading Ruth all the way to the park, around the "lake," and back home again while hopping on just three legs. And once again, after a few days, I began to look and feel like a normal, four-legged dog. But we knew that, at least for the next three months, caution and chondroitin would again be our top priority. Dr. G. encouraged us by telling us that he's seen dogs return to work and even participate in all sorts of competitions after an injury like mine.

We're expecting the best as I continue to recover and wait for the wagon. Meanwhile, I've earned my certification as a Canine Good Citizen and an International Therapy Dog. I'm just waiting for my photo ID to arrive in the mail.

I'm proud of this accomplishment, even though I must admit I wasn't always a model student. I liked to "cry wolf" and pretend I needed to do my business during class time, when I really just wanted to get out and sniff around (I only got away with this once or twice). And I caused Ruth some anxious moments during the certification test when I decided I'd rather *not* sit down as instructed. I also gobbled up my neighbor's dog biscuit as well as my own during the graduation celebration.

But the secret is perseverance. I went to school in the summer and in the fall, and I even took a winter class or two. I had to take one session twice—and that's fine. Things happen and setbacks occur. It's the way we handle them that makes all the difference.

My friend Molly, a beautiful white Maltese with adorable round eyes and a tail that fluffs out like a parasol, also wants to get certified. She hopes to bring love and smiles to nursing home residents. Like me, she's older, and she's also rescued—not from three upsetting weeks like I experienced, but from years of agony as a major producer in a puppy mill. She didn't quite make it in her first attempt at certification. She and her mom were very disappointed when she didn't pass one small part of the test, but guess what! Molly's going to try again.

They say that if a door closes, we should look for the open window. If the window also closes, then look to the Lord for guidance. Sometimes the best thing we can do is to just sit back and wait.

"Paws"
for Lessons Learned

Sing, even if (like Ruth) your voice isn't the greatest. It lifts the spirit.

Don't give up, and good things will happen.

Make the most of waiting time. Maybe even relax and enjoy it!

CHAPTER 12

Old Dog, New Tricks

They say you can't teach an old dog new tricks, but I don't believe it. With age comes wisdom—wisdom enough to not jump through all the hoops that come our way. But, when we want to, learning new tricks is a breeze.

Take, for example, that famous dog-actor, Benji. I heard that he was rescued from a shelter and made into a great movie star. He was no puppy, yet he learned lots of new tricks that endeared him to millions.

People, too, can learn new tricks when they're well past their formative years. The musical *My Fair Lady* is all about a poor apple-selling woman who is transformed into a lady of elegance. She learns a whole new way of speaking, and it changes her life completely. And what about all those older humans who have made outstanding contributions to the worlds of art, music, science, and literature?

Why, even cats can learn all sorts of things at an advanced age. Did you know that Ruth once had a performing cat? The cat wasn't on Broadway or anything like that, but she loved performing for friends and family. She was no spring kitten when she mastered those tricks, either. In case you've never heard of that cat, here's the scoop (*no pun intended*).

Ruth and Hugo took in an adult cat about 35 years ago. She wasn't really a stray, but a neighborhood cat who lived outside while her owners lavished most of their attention on their indoor dog, a gorgeous Irish setter. The cat had an adorable kitten, a little striped tiger who was the friendliest kitten ever. He would enthusiastically greet Ruth and Hugo as they went for their daily stroll. Sometimes he'd jump on Ruth's shoulder and enjoy the walk with them. He'd even come into their living room and visit. He was definitely one in a million—a "Mr. Purrr-sonality" if ever there was one!

Ruth and Hugo affectionately called the tiny feline "Mini," for obvious reasons. They just adored the little creature, and he them. But one day, the little guy wasn't there to greet and join them. Nor was he there the next day…or the next. When they encountered the owner of the cats, they naturally asked about Mini, but the owner said he hadn't seen him in a while either.

It was about then that Mini's mother started coming around to Ruth and Hugo's house. She, too, was of a beautiful tiger design, with thick, soft fur and lovely snow-white chest and paws. Ruth was sorry that she hadn't somehow tried to rescue Mini from his dangerous outdoor life, but at least now, she thought, she might be able to help Mini's mom. So she gave the older cat little treats and invited her into the house. The cat would creep in on cautious paws, always keeping an eye on the open door so she wouldn't feel trapped. If she got too far from her means of escape and sensed that the door might close, out she'd run.

Each time she'd visit she'd feel a little more at home, and one bitter cold day when Ruth came home from teaching her third-grade class, she followed Ruth right into the house as if she'd always lived there. Convinced that the cat had finally adopted them, Ruth and Hugo spoke with the owners, who were glad to accept some cash in exchange for the responsibility they hadn't taken very seriously anyway. Ruth named the cat Flavia, and the cat responded to that elegant name immediately.

The next day, Ruth had to stay home with a terrible cold (*probably from having the door open too much*). As she rested in bed, with Flavia snuggled nearby, an amazing thing happened. Ruth snoozed, and while in a dream-like state, she heard a cat purring. It was a special purr, one she recognized right away. It was Mini!

Upon awakening, Ruth felt certain that Mini was in heaven, happy that his mom was now their precious pet. Ruth spoke with all her heart to the little kitten, "Don't worry, Mini. We have your mom, and we'll take good care of her for you."

The neighbor rang the doorbell the very next day and told Ruth the sad news that Mini's body was found among the leaves in the gutter. A car had probably run him over. This confirmed what Ruth already knew in her heart and made her thankful, indeed, that Flavia now had a secure, loving home.

Flavia turned out to be a truly extraordinary cat who took great delight in learning new tricks. Ruth didn't purposely set out to create a performing cat, they both just loved to try new things. So it wasn't long before Flavia could roll over, shake hands, and make a little bell ring by hitting it first with one paw and then with the other. She'd jump up on their little green hassock, sit up, turn around, catch little rings thrown to her, and do a whole repertoire of fun things. It got so that whenever company came, she'd sit in the middle of the living room waiting for the chance to display her talents.

So, I tell you, dear friends, that older dogs (*as well as people and cats*) can indeed learn lots of new things. I think we're all grossly underestimated. Ruth recently told me that an expert on dogs says that we canines can learn at least one new word every week. It's a great way to keep our minds exercised, just as people do to ward off illnesses like Alzheimer's disease.

The teachers at my obedience school suspected that I already knew the words *heel, sit,* and *come* when I started the class. Of course I did! What did they expect? I wasn't born yesterday. I also came to Ruth knowing the word *stay*. This is a word I hate to hear as my people get ready to leave the house. I don't make a fuss and try to go with them; I just switch to my droopy-dog face and lower my tail. I still don't get to go, but it sure makes them feel guilty about leaving me.

When Ruth took me in, I also knew not to jump on people or furniture, to politely let my people go through a door or up the stairs ahead of me, and not to beg for people food. I knew not to bark unless it's absolutely necessary, like when a stranger rings the doorbell. Of course, I enjoy barking out of context every once in a while just to stymie people who can't for the life of them figure out why I'm barking!

Dogs like me, who come to a whole new environment later in life, need to be doubly smart. We not only need to learn a lot of new stuff, but we also have to unlearn some old stuff. When Ruth started pointing to the floor and saying, "Down," I'd automatically roll on my back for a tummy rub, as I'd always done. But it didn't take me long to realize that the rules had changed. This hand movement now means that I should lie down rightside up (*much to my tummy's dismay*).

It's fair to say that these past ten months have been a major learning experience for both Ruth and me. But our being seniors hasn't been a drawback. In fact, it's been an asset. We're at a stage in life where we possess an easygoing sense of humor and a philosophical optimism that makes it fun to learn new things. We learn so effortlessly sometimes that we don't even realize we're doing it.

One example of this is the way I've eased into relating new words to the actions that go with them. Now, as I trot in front of Ruth, all she has to say is "Left!" and I go left—or "Right!" and

I go right (and sometimes she says, "Which way?" and then *I* decide which route we'll take). Maybe someday I'll learn hand signals as well as words, like the dog we recently saw on television. The owner hid his dog's toy somewhere outside, and then directed the dog to find the toy, using only hand signals to tell the dog to go forward, back, right, and left. Isn't that amazing?

Ruth would also be thrilled if I could emulate a dog she saw on the International Therapy Dog video. The dog's owner sang ♫*How much is that doggie in the window...*♫ and the dog did the double-bark in all the right places. Of course, I don't bark much, no less bark on command. So I guess that trick will have to remain just a gleam in her eye, for the time being anyway.

Ruth bought a couple of books showing other fun tricks, and she, of course, comes up with some of her own. I'm quite able to learn them all, I'm just not sure I care to. We're still working on getting me to pick up my toy bones and put them in a basket. She thinks this would be funny and would show kids the importance of picking up litter or keeping their rooms neat. This isn't working so well because, as you know, I don't like to let go of my bones. She also likes me to wear a baseball cap while friends sing ♫ *Take me out to the ball game...*♫ That's an easy one—I just have to sit there. Of course, sitting there without shaking off the hat is quite a trick!

The trick I like best is when I choose which hand has the treat. Flavia did that one, too. And, like Flavia, I create some tricks of my own. She did her own high-altitude tricks, like running on the roof of the house, jumping onto the top of the refrigerator from a standstill, napping between the drop ceiling and the original ceiling, and running up the pull-down attic stairs. No cat since Flavia has even *tried* to go up those stairs—and I'll surely not!

But I have an amazing Houdini-like trick. I surprise people with it sometimes if I have to sit in the car for too long. I miraculously get out of my seat belt harness and sit there proudly, letting them know who's in control—and making them wonder how I could escape while leaving the harness still attached to the seat belt!

And I even go a step further than Flavia by sometimes getting Ruth and Hugo to jump through hoops. I let Hugo know in no uncertain terms when I prefer to wait and walk with Ruth rather than with him. She's more lenient and patient, letting me choose where we'll walk and allowing me to sniff to my nose's content. I have also trained them to spoil me on occasion with their great home cooking, my favorite dish being the ground bison with a touch of pasta, veggies, and tomato sauce. Heaven!

Old dogs, new tricks? Not a problem here. In fact, let me tell you a little secret…

I can't wait to see what I'll be learning next!

"Paws"
for Lessons Learned

Expect to keep on learning and you'll see lots of opportunities.

Greet each day with eager anticipation. Try something new.

Encourage others to try new things, too. Try some together!

CHAPTER 13

Dogged Determination

How do you suppose the term "dogged determination" came into being? I have no doubt that these two words fit so nicely together because determined is what we dogs are. Just take a good look at us:

- Our canine ancestors decided to forge a friendship with humans second to none. And now only the dog has the honor of being called "People's Best Friend."

- Dogs are selected to perform arduous, high-concentration tasks like pulling sleds in snowstorms, searching for lost people, and selflessly dedicating their lives to guiding sightless people.

- Dogs are now given the awesome responsibility of sniffing out cancer cells, bombs, and illegal drugs so that people can have safer and healthier lives.

- Dogs like me have learned how to identify bogus CDs, and because this is such a dangerous business, they need bodyguards to protect them from dealers who are now out to get them.

- My species has served gallantly in the armed forces, helping soldiers to sidestep hidden grenades and alerting them to impending dangers that only dogs can hear or sense.

- Dogs are trained to rescue drowning people, work with convicts, and help disabled children.

And the list goes on and on.

Our loyal and tenacious spirit is lauded in books like *The Incredible Journey* and films about Lassie and Rin Tin Tin. We're stubborn, persistent, and lavishly faithful, all qualities that endear us to humans in a way that no other animal on earth can match.

It was my own dogged determination that kept me going through that hardship of losing my family after so many years together. It also served me well in adjusting to my new home and even in writing this book.

It's my determined spirit that keeps me sniffing through the leaves until I finally latch on to that old discarded chicken bone that's buried at the bottom. And it's the same spirit that prompts me to relinquish it when Ruth frantically shouts, "Leave it!" I'm more determined to do her proud than to hold on to what I want.

I know I've been adopted into a life of service as well as a life of fun and games. And I'm determined to do my best to find the good—in myself, in others, and in the world—and to keep it growing and showing. The great thing about determination, especially *dogged* determination, is that the more we exert it, the more we see things fall right into place.

I no sooner finished telling you about waiting for my wagon than the wagon appeared. And with it came my new friends, Lindsay and Melissa. They found out that I was waiting for a wagon when their mom, Lisa, read about me in the local paper. And they offered me theirs. It's a colorful, kid-friendly wagon that's both lightweight and strong.

Although they're just eleven years old, Melissa and Lindsay are already talented artists, writers, and actresses, and they enjoy working with small children. They're going to help us plan events and projects that will make people more aware of animals and children in need of loving homes. And since I've "been there, done that" in terms of needing a home, I'm voted in as the poster girl for these projects.

Jeff and Mark, my friends at the nearby service station who keep the family cars in good running order, have customized my "*Waggin' Wagon*" so we can all safely enjoy it. They've designed a sturdy yet comfortable pulling system for me. Next will come the seat belts (*safety first!*) and then some lettering on the sides. The final touch is a black, furry wagging tail made by our clever and versatile friend, Marge (the garage sale guru). The tail goes on the back of the wagon to make it a one-of-a-kind wagon that really wags!

I expect that lots of people will help us as we move ahead with our various activities. And you can be sure we'll be doggedly determined to work together in fun-filled ways that are beneficial to all concerned.

I now have my therapy dog photo ID and am starting to visit folks in a nearby nursing home. I recently did a 1.5-mile cancer walk with my good friend Martha, helping a little to pull her wheelchair. My friends Adam and Daniel let me try pulling them, one at a time, in my wagon. Then *they* pulled *me!* And when Max, Julian and Sean, my closest (right next door) friends come over to play with me, they also read to me. They're teaching me to be a good listener so someday I can be an official "reading dog" for a school or library.

I thank God every day for my new life, my new friends, my new goals…and the dogged determination that enables me to walk, *even run*, boldly and joyfully into the future.

"Paws"
for Lessons Learned

If there's something good you want to do, go for it!

Think of (and do for) others. It adds meaning to our lives.

Maintain a grateful heart. It attracts happiness like a magnet.

Bark up the Right Tree

CHAPTER 14

I Have a Dream!

In fact, I have many dreams. Little dreams that add spice to every day, and big dreams that go far beyond my next meal or the next car ride. They even extend beyond my life here on earth. For example:

I see people of all ages enjoying this book. They laugh at the funny parts, cry at the sad parts, and when they put it down, they find creative ways to save the animals and children who find themselves homeless through no fault of their own.

I see Kids 'n' Kritters thriving as one of those creative solutions—a place where adoptive families can get a good start by learning and applying love-filled principles in a supportive environment.

I see my Maltese friend Molly, myself, and countless other rescued dogs finding delightful ways to return the love for which we are now so thankful.

I see big, juicy, canine kisses (and loving feline licks) tickling the noses of people whose hearts have led them to rescue these wonderful pets.

I see children who were once homeless and without their families finding the security of a new home and a loving "forever family."

I see courageous people reaching out to ease the pain of people and animals in distant places, as well as right here in our own country.

I see myself taking part in inspiring causes, raising funds, and making guest appearances. Why not? We don't pass this way again, so now is our chance to make a difference.

It took the combined efforts of many wonderful people and selfless volunteers to get me to where I am today. And I'm just one of the 250,000 animals on the Petfinder website!

There's lots of work to be done on so many fronts. It's easy to get overwhelmed, discouraged, and even dog-tired just thinking about the many challenges, but I envision people working together, using their time, talents, and treasures in far-reaching ways:

- *people who clearly see what really matters and make amazing headway against all odds,*
- *people who know the score and aren't easily misled or intimidated,*
- *people who love the Lord and love others as themselves,*
- *people who enthusiastically follow their hearts,*
- *people who truly...*

BARK up the RIGHT Tree.

And I invite *YOU* to be one of them.

"Paws"
for Lessons Learned

Make a positive difference. Our contributions, no matter how small, can have huge effects.

Thank those who have helped and inspired you, while you can. If it's too late, honor them with actions that would please them.

Go ahead and dream. All types of dreams, both big and small, can and do come true!

Woof! Woof!

ACKNOWLEDGEMENTS

W*oof! Woof!* Sure hope you liked my book. It was written especially for you, dear readers. But as you well know, I didn't write it alone. I must thank Ruth for being my voice and the wind beneath my paws.

And it wasn't just Ruth and me. We had a whole pack of pals involved in this canine memoir. Without them, our book wouldn't be what it is today. So we would like to express, from the bottom of our hearts, the thanks due to so many.

Lisa Matalon, accolades to you for your great ideas and uplifting additions, including the little heart on the front cover. We greatly appreciate the time and expertise it took for you to edit and improve the manuscript.

Hugo and Elisa, our family editors. We can't thank you enough for the many contributions you made to the project.

You lovingly held our nose and snout to the grindstone, showing us again and again that it can always be better.

Thanks also to *you*, Hedy Lewenstein and Laurie Kaplan, for your input and editing skills. And to Jessica Radzak, our professional editor, for giving this manuscript a final look-over and making a world of difference.

A round of applause for Victoria Vinton of Coyote Press Graphics, (www.coyotepressgraphics.com), our amazing graphic artist. You put together a fantastic cover, devised a great layout for the text, and worked wonders with the photos, including the one of my very own paw!

And a hearty thank-you to all the people and pets who were the players in our story—the ones who made it all happen. You can now start thinking about who should portray you in the movie. Vinny, you'll have to play yourself because no movie star can do you justice!

Special thanks to my original family for my many years with you. Endless wags and kisses to Denise, Lisa, and everyone at Rawhide Rescue in Warren, New Jersey. And let's not forget our loving God who brought it all together and continues to guide and bless us.

Now it's up to you, dear friends, to turn just one more page and add your bark to mine as we stretch toward that love which never *ever* fails.

"Paws"
for Consideration

Ways to ease the pain for animals and children in need:

- Welcome one (or more) into your home. For pets, go to websites like Petfinder, or visit local shelters and rescue groups to see who might be there, waiting just for you. To help children, search out websites like ABC News: Kids Who Need Homes, AdoptUsKids, Children's Aid & Family Services (www.cafsnj.org; New Jersey only), and a host of others that specialize in placing children in good homes.

- Support causes that are dear to your heart. Volunteer. Make a donation. Do both! When you give of yourself, you provide something no one else can. When you give money, you encourage and enable those on the front line who are working hard to remedy problems and make dreams come true.

- Walk a dog whose owner is ill, mentor a nearby child, or write to a faraway child through an organization like World Vision. Anything you do to help an animal or child is a bark in the right direction and an investment in the future.

- Spread the word. Pass this book on to others. Give it as a gift, loan it out, or simply recommend it. The more who read it, the more the kids and critters will benefit.

Ten percent of the proceeds from this book will go to charities that help animals and children in need—including *Kids 'n' Kritters*, the dream that's just waiting to come true. As our dream becomes reality we invite you to follow our progress by noting our news and updates on *www.opendoorsagf.org*.

Right now, we plan to sell custom-made buttons and magnets with pictures of beloved pets. My 11-year-old friends, Melissa and Lindsay, are writing a skit for the new dramatic group they've organized called the Bow-WOW Bunch! We've already made Chapter 9 into a musical melodrama and are planning to take it "on the road" to promote adoptions. And we have a big gleam in our eyes that one day soon we'll have our own annual DogFest, which will be a fun-filled, one-of-a-kind fundraiser.

Please put your good ideas into action as you read this book and ponder the paws. Think of each and every paw as a "high four" to encourage and thank you. And don't forget to e-mail me at *Jessiesfriends@verizon.net* to tell me about all the good things going on in your life (and in the lives of others *because* of you). Let's see how much of a difference we can make!

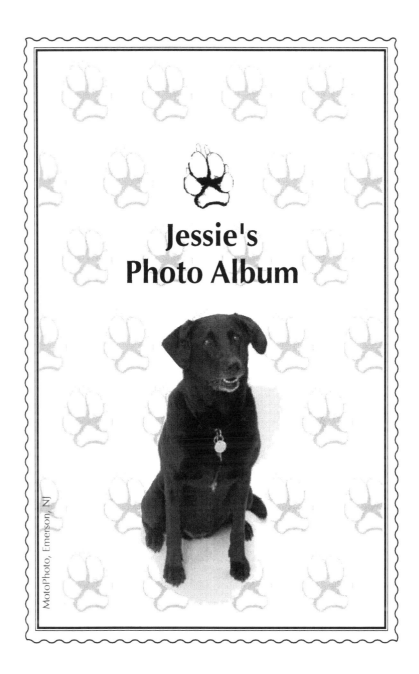

Jessie's
Photo Album

MotoPhoto, Emerson, NJ

Ruth & Me

Hugo & me on a hike

Molly & me (Ch. 11)

Me recuperating (Ch. 10)

Vinny, Cilia, Madison, and Tony (Ch. 7)

Michael & Maggie (Ch. 8)

Daniel in my Waggin' Wagon

Ruth, Elisa & Denise (Ch 4)

Sunbathing with Annabelle

My idea of swimming (Ch. 6)

My reading buddy Sean

Julian & me

Maryan presents my diploma.

Adam & me, with my squeaky bone

My pals Melissa & Lindsay (Ch. 13)

Artie & Jett (Ch. 10)

Me & Dr. G.

My Waggin' Wagon (that's not my tail!)

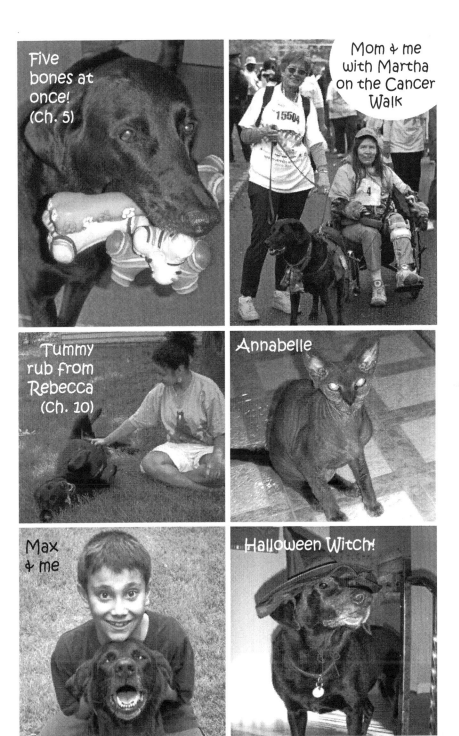

Lessons from a Rescued Dog

To Molly...

This book is dedicated to our dear friend Molly, who died of congestive heart failure just after this book was written. Molly had a very sad and difficult life, giving birth to countless litters in an illegal puppy mill.

During the past three years, however, she finally found the happiness she so deserved. She was rescued by Metropolitan Maltese Rescue in New York City, and adopted by Kathleen and John, who absolutely adored her.

She did not get to bring joyful smiles to nursing home residents as she had hoped (Chapter 11), but she left a legacy of love with all who knew her. And she asks us to remember her by reaching out to others in need of rescue.